Workbook

New International Edition

Grade 2

Tara Lievesley, Deborah Herridge
Series editor: John Stringer

PEARSON

ALWAYS LEARNING

Pearson Education Limited is a company incorporated in England and Wales having its registered office at Edinburgh Gate, Harlow, Essex, CM20 2JE.

Registered company number: 872828

Text © Pearson Education Limited 2012

First published 2003. This edition published 2012.

www.pearsonglobalschools.com

20 19 18

IMP 10 9 8 7

British Library Cataloguing in Publication Data
A catalogue record for this book is available from the British Library

ISBN 978 0 43513 370 2

Edited by Janice Curry

Designed by Ian Foulis

Original illustrations © Pearson Education Limited, 2003, 2009, 2012

Illustrated by Ian Foulis and Steve Evans

The publisher would like to thank the following for their kind permission to reproduce their photographs:

Cover photo/illustration © Charles McClean, Alamy Images

(Key: b- bottom; C- Center; l-left; l-right; t-top)

Alamy Image: 42cr; Shutterstock.com:29bl, 29bl, Picsfive 26tr

All other image © pearson Education

Printed in the UK by CPI Colour

Acknowledgements
Every effort has been made to contact copyright holders of material reproduced in this book. Any omissions will be rectified in subsequent printings if notice is given to the publishers.

Contents

Let's explore!

Draw an animal you find in each habitat.

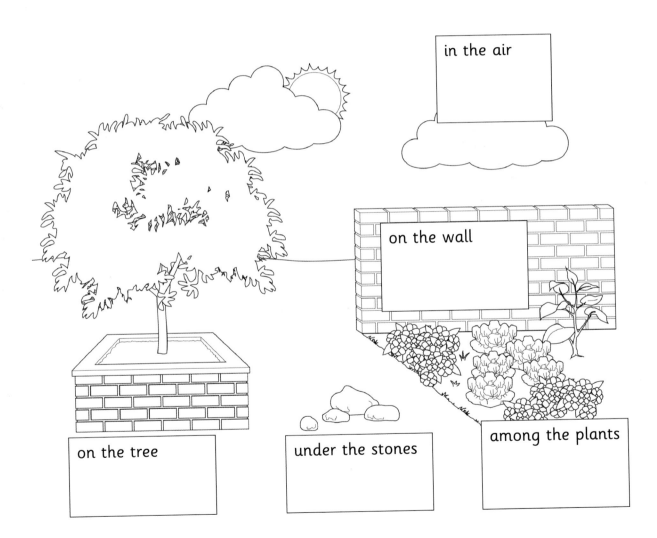

in the air

on the wall

on the tree

under the stones

among the plants

WS 2 Look closely

Look carefully at one animal or plant you have found.

Draw what you see.

Label what you have drawn.

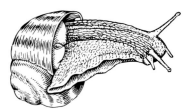

Snail

Flower

Home sweet home

1 The place an animal lives is called its _____.

2 Who lives here? Add animals to their habitats.

In the desert

Under the sea

Rainforest habitat

Finish this drawing of the rainforest. Include as many animals and plants as you can.

Living things

Circle the animals that live in the water **blue**.

Circle the animals that do not live in water **red**.

Not everything here is an animal.

Minibeasts around school

Class 2 hunted for minibeasts. This is what they found.

Minibeast	spider	ant	scorpion	beetle	dragonfly	fly
Number	1	14	0	4	0	2

They have started their graph. Finish it for them. Give it a title.

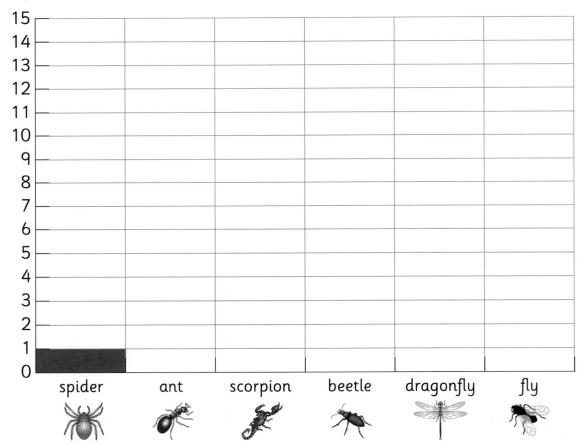

How many minibeasts did they find altogether? _____

Minibeasts

1 Count the legs on each animal.

2 Write the number of legs next to it.

3 Insects have six legs. How many are insects? ☐

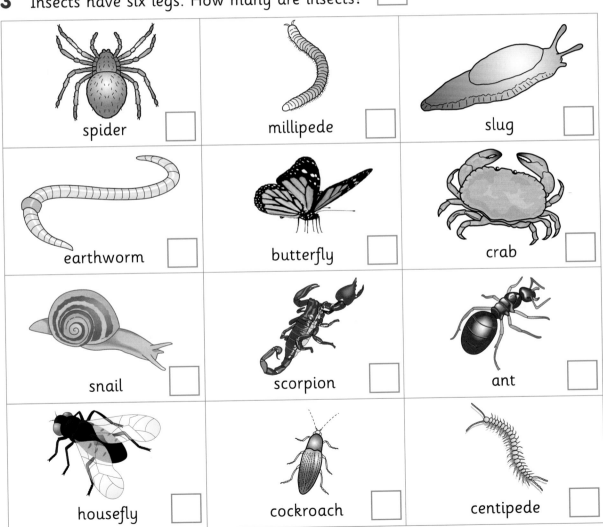

spider ☐	millipede ☐	slug ☐
earthworm ☐	butterfly ☐	crab ☐
snail ☐	scorpion ☐	ant ☐
housefly ☐	cockroach ☐	centipede ☐

Minibeast identification key

ant   centipede   butterfly   spider

Look at the animals above. Use the key and Worksheet 7 to identify them.

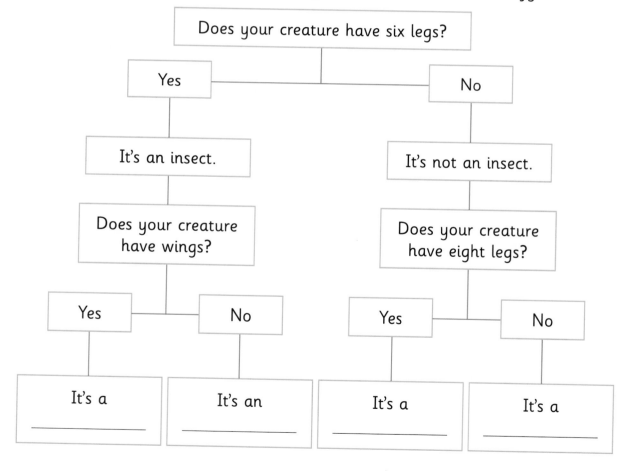

Does your creature have six legs?

| Yes | No |

It's an insect.   It's not an insect.

Does your creature have wings?   Does your creature have eight legs?

| Yes | No | | Yes | No |

It's a _____   It's an _____   It's a _____   It's a _____

WS 9

All change

Throw a dice. Move a counter. Follow the rules.

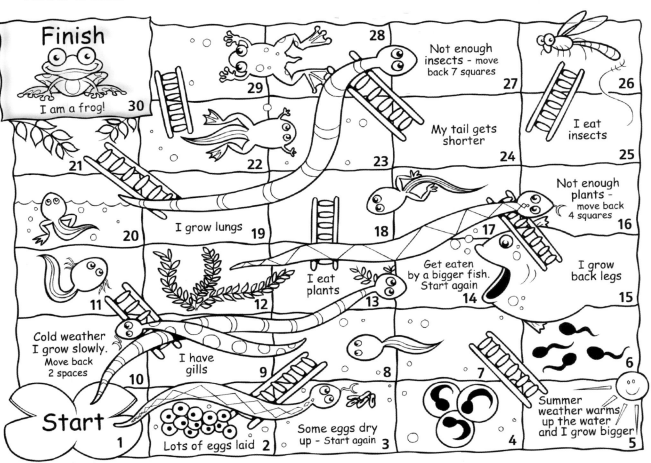

Who finishes first? _____

Caring for our environment

Write things you could do to care for your environment.

I could stop:

1 _____

2 _____

3 _____

4 _____

I could start to:

1 _____

2 _____

3 _____

4 _____

The weather

What is the weather like? Fill in the weather diary below using the symbols.

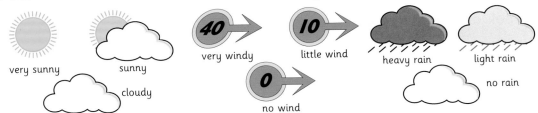

very sunny

sunny

cloudy

very windy

little wind

no wind

heavy rain

light rain

no rain

Day	Sun	Wind	Rain
1			
2			
3			
4			
5			

Unit 1 assessment

1 The place an animal or plant lives is called its _____ .

2 Look at these pictures. Draw lines to connect each animal to where it lives.

f_____   b_____   s_____   b_____   g_____

3 Write the names of the animals underneath their pictures.

4 Sort the animals. How many legs does each animal have?
Write two in each box.

No legs	Six legs	More than six legs
earthworm		

WS 13 Materials from the earth

All these materials are found in the earth.

Draw a line joining the description to the material's use.

Draw another line from the use to the picture.

sandstone

1 Black, hard, dirty

used to make bricks

diamond

2 White, hard, smooth

marks the schoolboard

marble

3 Sticky, squashy

used for fuel

clay

4 Hard, red or yellow

used for jewellery

chalk

5 White, soft

used for statues

coal

6 Clear and shiny, very expensive

used for buildings

WS 14 Scratch testing

Kofi was testing rocks.

He wanted to find which rock was the hardest.

These are his results.

Rock number		It was scratched by rock number		
		1	2	3
	1	X	no	no
	2	yes	X	no
	3	yes	yes	X

1 Which number rock was the hardest? _____

2 Which number rock was the softest? _____

3 Rock number 1 was granite.
Rock number 2 was soapstone.
Rock number 3 was clay.
Write the names of the rocks in order, hardest first:

_____ _____ _____ _____

4 How many of these rocks would a diamond scratch? _____

Matching materials

Match the material with where it comes from and what it is made into.

For example:

sheep   ball of wool   woollen jumper

tea plant

cotton thread

butter

duck

tea bag

glass bottle

wheat

flour

cup of tea

cow

glass

T-shirt

sand

milk

pillow

cotton plant

feathers

bread

WS 16

Natural or artificial?

How many different materials can you name?

Make two lists. The pictures will help you.

Natural materials	Artificial materials
wood	nylon

Will it change?

Write yes or no in each box for each material.

Material	Will it bend?	Will it stretch?	Will it twist?
Elastic band			yes
Plasticine			
Aluminium foil		no	
Cookie dough			

WS 18 Marvellous mixtures

Write the recipe for your chocolate crispy cakes here:

Ingredients (what you need)

_____

_____

_____

_____

Method (what you need to do)

First_____

_____

Then _____

_____

Then_____

_____

Draw a picture of your finished cakes.

Dissolving substances

Amina and Khalifa are investigating.

They want to find out which substances dissolve in water.

Can you help them?

Find some substances and fill in the table.

substance	Add cold water	What the water looks like
salt	disappeared after stirring	clear

Name: _____ Date: _____

Unit 2 assessment

1 You can easily squeeze or squash these materials. True or false?

rubber _____   stone _____

wood _____   brick _____

plastic _____   wool _____

metal _____

2 Join the material to where it comes from.

leather   comes from the ground.

coal   comes from a sheep.

wool   comes from trees.

wood   comes from a cow.

glass   comes from a plant.

cotton   is made from sand.

3 Choose what happens when you warm these things. Circle the word.

⬤ dough	melts	cooks	hardens
⬤ chocolate	hardens	freezes	melts
⬤ clay	burns	hardens	melts
⬤ wax	cooks	melts	hardens
⬤ ice	hardens	cooks	melts

4 Write one use of granite. _____

Sources of light

Circle the light sources.

Sun   candle   reflective strip   pencil   bonfire
                              on coat

TV   hat   light bulb   mirror

Draw one more light source.

A sunny day

Circle all the things in the picture that protect us from the Sun.

Write three things we do to keep us safe in the Sun.

1 _____

2 _____

3 _____

WS 23

Sun safety

Design a poster to remind us to keep safe in the Sun.

WS 24 Brightness

All of these are sources of light.

Label them from 1 to 4, with 1 being the dimmest and 4 being the brightest.
Name them.

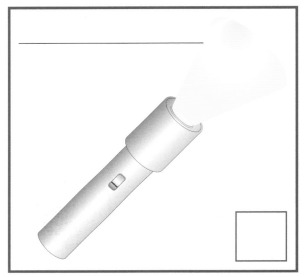

_____

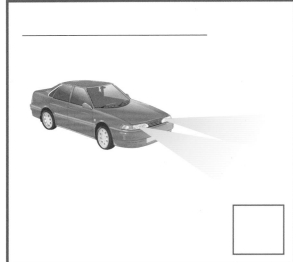

_____

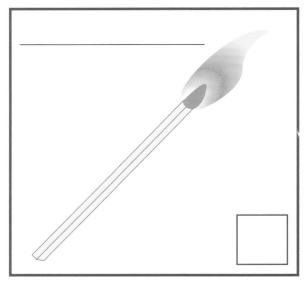

_____

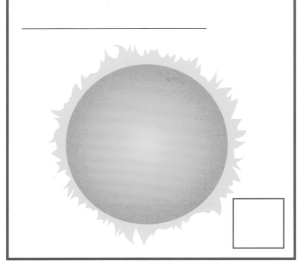

_____

Name that shadow

These are the shadows of things in the kitchen.

Write the name of each one.

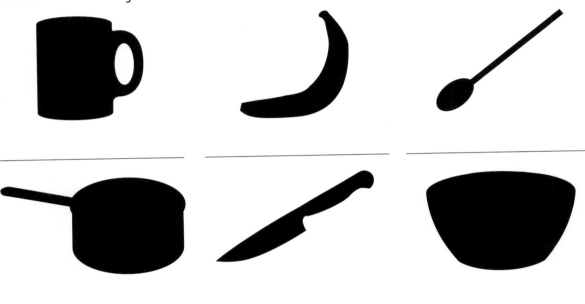

_____   _____   _____

_____   _____   _____

Now draw an object you would find in your classroom.

Draw what its shadow looks like.

Sorting materials

Saad and Noor want to sort these materials.

Tick the ones that will make strong shadows.

card

plastic pop bottle

aluminium foil

wooden chopping board

cotton T-shirt

bubble wrap

milk carton

plastic bag

glass beaker

leather belt

Write down two other objects that would make strong shadows.

_____

_____

Changing shadows

Saad and Noor have made a shadow puppet.

Explain why the puppet makes a shadow.

_____

_____

_____

_____

Where would Noor need to hold the puppet to make the shadow bigger? Mark a place on the picture with a cross.

Name: _____ Date: _____

WS 28 My shadow

Maalik walks to school and back.

His shadows are different at different times of the day.

1 Draw the missing shadows in the second picture as Maalik goes home at 2.00 p.m.

2 Draw the Sun in the right place in the second picture.

3 Maalik's shadow is different because _____

_____

WS 29

Unit 3 assessment 1

1 Tick three light sources.

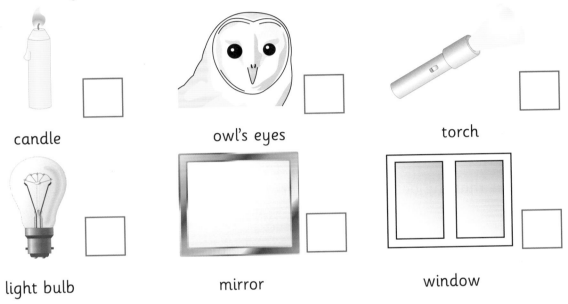

candle ☐   owl's eyes ☐   torch ☐

light bulb ☐   mirror ☐   window ☐

2 We see the Sun in the daytime and the Moon at night. Which is a light source? Tick the light source.

☐   ☐

WS 30 Unit 3 assessment 2

3 Tick the right answer.

The Sun's light can hurt your eyes because:

a) it is so bright ❏

b) it shines all day ❏

c) it is a light source ❏

4 Hassan was exploring the cave. What could he take to help him to see?

_____

5 Why is that the best thing to take?

_____

6 Draw where Safia's shadow will be on the picture.

Electricity at home

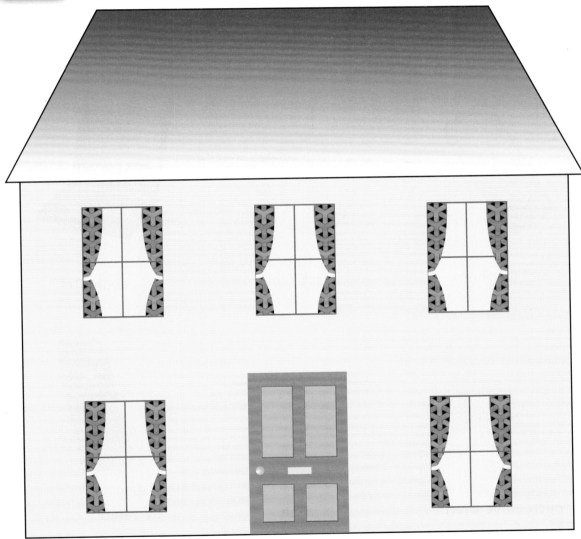

1 Draw, or write, things upstairs that use batteries.

2 Draw, or write, things downstairs that use mains electricity.

WS 32 Electricity 1

Look at the objects on these two pages.

Tick (✓) the things that need mains electricity to work.

Circle the things that use battery electricity.

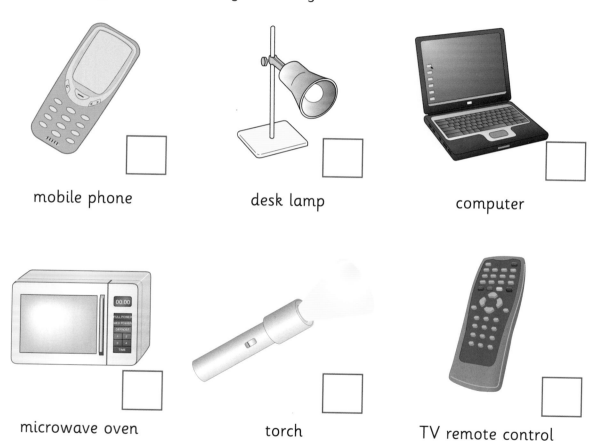

| mobile phone | desk lamp | computer |

| microwave oven | torch | TV remote control |

Electricity 2

Tick (✓) the things that need electricity to work.

Circle the things that use battery electricity.

grandfather pendulum clock ☐

cup ☐

pencil ☐

game controller ☐

camera ☐

remote controlled car ☐

electric drill ☐

sunglasses ☐

Mains electricity can be dangerous

WS 34

Circle all the dangers.

Name: _____ Date: _____

WS 35

Helpful electricity

Design an electrical robot to do the work that you don't like doing.

Write about what it does and how it works.

WS 36 Circuits

Will each bulb light? Put a tick (✓) in the box if you think it will.

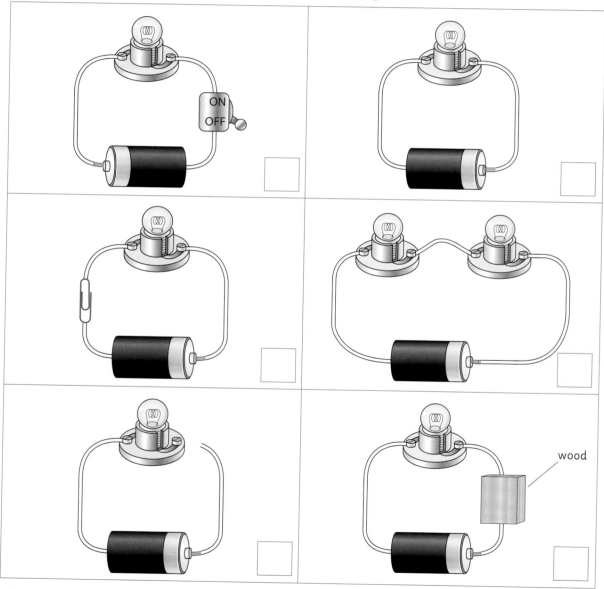

How would you make the other circuits work?

A complete circuit

Tick (✓) the complete circuits.

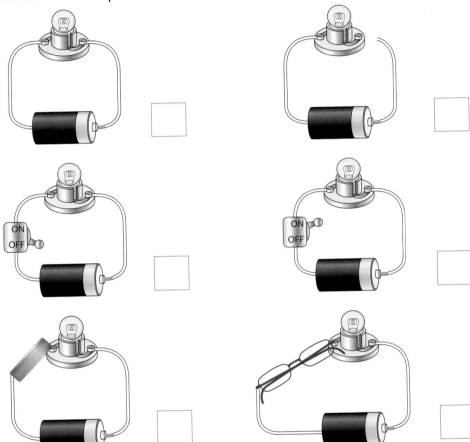

Why don't the other circuits work?

_____

_____

_____

WS 38 How do you use electricity? 1

Draw or write how you use electricity during the day.

Morning

Afternoon

How do you use electricity? 2

Draw or write how you use electricity during the day and night.

Evening

Night

Making models

Design your electrical model here.

How many components will you use?

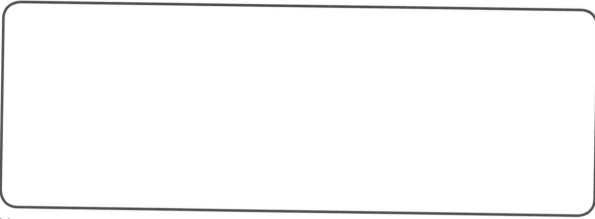

What must your circuit look like? Draw it here.

Apprentice electrician

Here are some circuits that do not work.

What do you need to do to make them work?

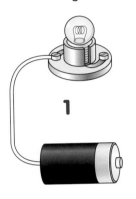

1

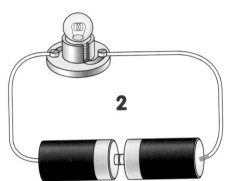

2

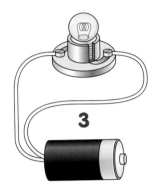

3

Draw the correct circuits.

Name: _____   Date: _____

WS 42 Symbols

These are the symbols electricians use to draw diagrams of circuits.

—|⊢—	—⊗—	———	—Ⓜ—	buzzer	—∘⁄∘—
battery	bulb	wire	motor	buzzer	switch

Draw some other examples of symbols you might see around you, and say what they mean.

This is telling you to keep safe!

Here's one from the *Student Book*.

WS 43

Unit 4 assessment

1 Write three things that use mains electricity.

_____

_____

_____

2 Write three things that use a battery.

_____

_____

_____

3 Look at the circuit pictures.

Tick (✓) which circuits will work.

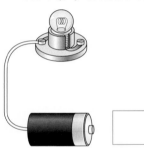  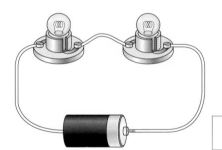

4 Draw a picture of a complete circuit with a bulb and a switch.

WS 44 Earth and beyond

This is a diagram of our solar system.

Label the Sun and the missing planets.

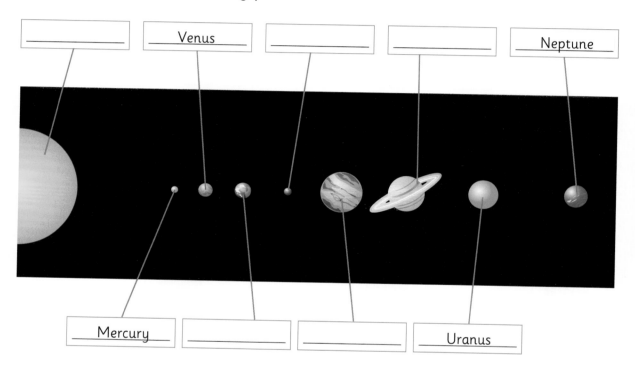

| _____ | Venus | _____ | _____ | Neptune |

Mercury | _____ | _____ | Uranus

Use these words to help you.

Earth   Jupiter   Mars   Saturn   Sun

WS 45 Postcard from another world

Imagine you have travelled to a planet in another galaxy.

Complete the address to send a postcard home.

Design a postage stamp from your new planet .

Milky Way

Universe

Long and short

The length of shadows changes during the day.

At the beginning of the day shadows are _____

In the middle of the day shadows are _____

At the end of the day shadows are _____

Here are some photos that Dana took.

Which were taken in the middle of the day?

WS 47

Moving shadows

Tamara is measuring the shadow
of a shadow stick.

She measures the shadow each hour. She has written her results in a table.

Time	7am	8am	9am	10am	11am	12noon	1pm	2pm	3pm
Shadow length (cm)	80	70	50	20	5	20	50	70	90

Tamara has started a bar chart to show the lengths of shadows. Finish it
for her. Give it a title.

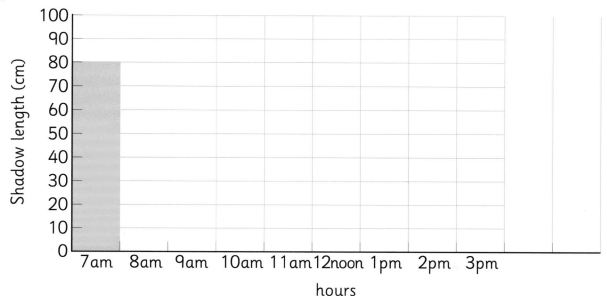

What's another year?

It takes a whole year for the Earth to travel round the Sun.

Write or draw what happens in each month of the year in this solar diagram.

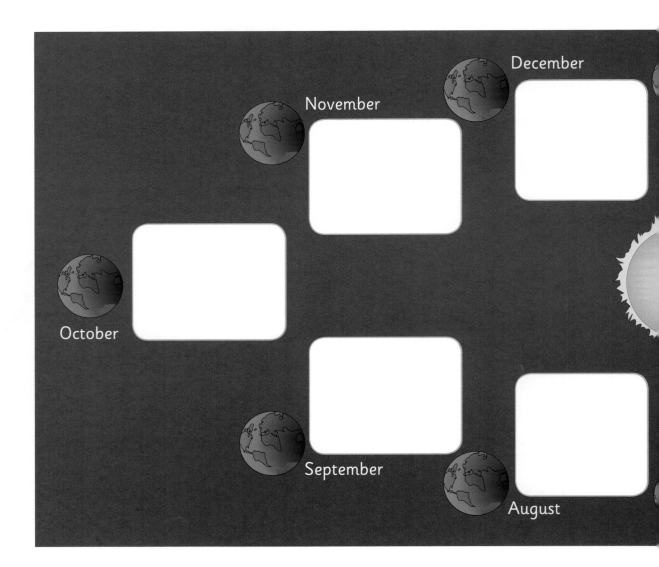

In which month is your birthday?

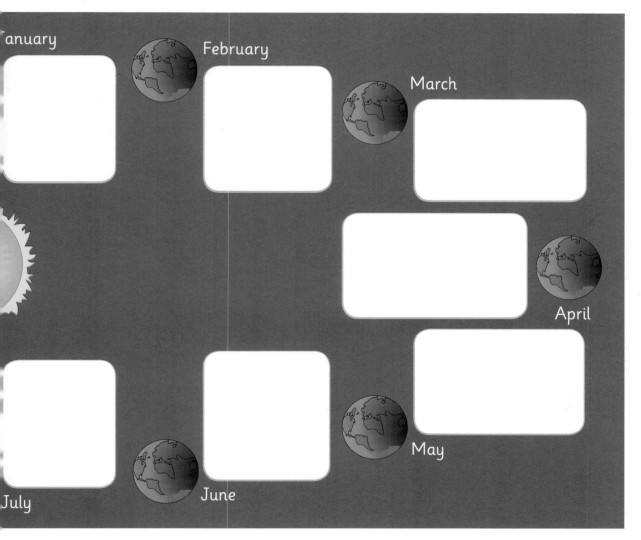

Night and day

This picture shows a diagram of the Earth seen from space.

- Shade the section of the Earth where it is night.
- Draw a person on part of the Earth where it is day. Draw their shadow.

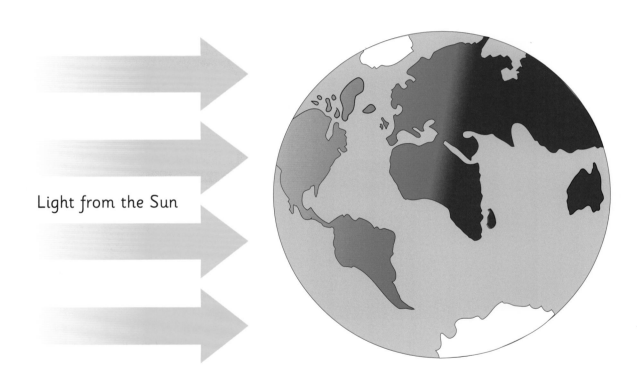

Light from the Sun

How long does it take for the Earth to spin round once? _____

WS 50

Unit 5 assessment

1 Nabila's little brother is making a model of the Earth, Sun and Moon. He has collected some things.

Draw a line to the best choice.

PE hoop

dinner plate

tennis ball

football

golf ball

paper plate

marble

beach ball

Earth

Sun

Moon

2 Complete the sentences.

Use these words to help you: **East   West   Sun   spins**

The Earth we live on _____ around. This makes it look to us as

if the _____ is moving. During the day it seems to move from

_____ to _____.

3 How long does it take the Earth to spin once? _____

4 How long does it take the Earth to travel once around the Sun?

_____